MW01247438

Elon Musk

A Biography of Innovator, Entrepreneur,
and Billionaire Elon Musk

Table of Contents

Introduction

Elon Musk is the CEO of SpaceX, one of the leading lights at Tesla, and the head honcho of many other companies. Unless you have been living in a cave since 1995, chances are you know at least a little about this South African born entrepreneur. He is a prolific Twitter user, and this has been a source of amusement for some and downright offensive to others. Trouble seems to follow him, and yet he remains successful. One thing we do know about Elon Musk is he is never boring! His spats with authorities and rival tech billionaires are legendary, and they provide the media with endless content to entertain their subscribers.

His successes are many. Electric vehicles, space tourism, the colonization of Mars, and connecting computers to the human brain may all sound like something straight from a sci-fi novel, but Musk is the man who has dedicated his life to making them come true. Love him or loathe him; you will always find it interesting to see what makes him tick. Why is he so hell-bent on changing the future? This book will give you a glimpse into the life of the man who is referred to as the real-life Iron Man, Elon Musk.

Chapter 1: The Childhood Story of Elon Musk

On the 28th of June in 1971, the eldest child of successful couple Errol and Maye Musk was born. His arrival into the world at Pretoria in South Africa is the starting point of the story of one of the most important figures of the technological age. As he grew up alongside two other younger siblings, brother Kimbal and younger sister Tosca, he was an avid thinker and prone to introversion. Young Elon was so intense that his mother Maye feared he was partially deaf.

At school, Elon studied hard but was the subject of bullying due to his inability to fit in with the other children. One attack was so severe he was thrown down a flight of stairs, and his nose was broken as his head hit the pavement. He was hospitalized following the attack, and his nose still bears the scars he sustained. He later had to have treatment to repair a jagged spectrum that troubled his breathing due to the attack.

Life with His Parents

Errol and Maye Musk met in high school. They married in 1970 and produced three children, Elon, Kimbal, and Tosca. To the outside world, they seemed like the perfect family with perfect parents and a wealthy home life. Errol was working as an engineer and earning good money, while Maye started her career in the modeling industry. However, within the family home, all was not well.

Errol was an irresponsible father who often turned to extramarital affairs to keep his sexual interest peaked, and he later admitted to being a failure as a father. It is believed that Maye wanted to leave Errol due to physical and mental abuse within the marriage but failed to do so because the divorce laws of South Africa didn't favor the wife. Eventually, she left the family home and escaped to Canada with her daughter. The two boys were given a choice to leave with their mother or stay with their father in South Africa. They chose to continue to live in Pretoria with their father, but they soon realized their mistake.

Despite being successful in business and owning an emerald mine in Zambia, he didn't provide child support to his wife in Canada. He also treated his boys cruelly and failed to support their efforts at school and home. Despite Elon already having sold his first business, a software game called Blastar, for $500 by the age of 12, he was constantly belittled by his father. He and his brother were told they could never amount to anything, and Elon has later described his childhood as miserable.

In the late 1980s, the two boys rejoined their mother in Canada. This is the period when the strength and resilience of Maye Musk emerged! She often worked multiple jobs at a time to raise her kids and fulfill their basic needs. She worked as a dietician and traveled from practice to practice across Canada while picking up modeling jobs on the way. She also taught nutrition at a college in the evenings to help to pay the bills.

She chose to remain single, unlike her ex-husband, and once told an interviewer that she was worried about going on a date just in case they split the bill. This fear of being unable to feed her kids kept her mind focused on her achievements as well as her children's.

Errol was not so focused on staying single. He met and married a widowed lady called Heidi Mari, who already had three children from her previous marriage, including 4-year-old Jana, Jock junior, and Harry. They went on to have two more children together, named Ali and Rose. As the marriage flourished, so did Errol's wealth. He became a real estate developer and went on to own even more mining shares in Zambia.

The family lived a prosperous and seemingly happy life at the many luxurious properties they owned. Errol had a passion for thoroughbred horses and would travel between stables in his Cessna aircraft, which he enjoyed piloting himself. He also boasted a private yacht, and the family loved to holiday together on board. Life was not all holidays and happiness, though. Errol continued his philandering, and the couple eventually divorced around 2010 when Heidi learned of an extramarital relationship that finally tipped the scales.

The period that followed was when it got tricky for Elon and Errol to maintain a civil relationship. The news was leaked that Errol had fathered a child with his stepdaughter Jana after initially hiding the relationship from the public. He claimed that the relationship began following a tumultuous break up between Jana and a former boyfriend. This child was initially believed to be the product of the former relationship, but paternity tests showed that Errol was the father. It was shown that this scandalous revelation was the reason behind the breakup of the marriage.

Errol was also accused of manslaughter following a shooting incident at his home in Pretoria. Three intruders were shot and killed by Musk, but he maintained he was acting in self-defense and was acquitted with a clean slate.

The New Addition to the Family

It's safe to say that nobody was breaking out celebratory cigars as news of the birth of Errol's sixth child was announced. Reports suggest that Elon "went berserk" at the news that his father and stepsister were expecting a baby. He went public with the news of his estrangement from his father in the same year, but he didn't specify the reason for it. While the estrangement could have been for several reasons, it's fair to assume that the birth of Elliot Musk would have added to the tension between Errol and Elon.

In an interview with the magazine Rolling Stone, he described his father as "evil" and accused him of being a "terrible human being." He went on to describe his father as a criminal and accused him of committing every evil act that people could imagine. The interview was a highly emotional experience and had Elon openly crying. The sight of one of the most powerful men in the world with tears running down his cheeks was one of the most disturbing images of the year, but how did it affect his father?

Errol has also been quite vocal about the split between himself and his son. He accuses Elon of being a "spoilt brat" and accused him of being immature. He believed that the shooting incident was the reason Elon reacted as he did rather than the new addition to the family. He described his new son Elliot as "perfect" and a "gift from God."

In an interview with a British newspaper, he described an idyllic childhood where he drove his kids to school in a Rolls Royce Corniche and described the horses and motorbikes his children had at an early age. He speculates that maybe he spoilt his kids, and that's what caused Elon to act the way he did during the

Rolling Stone interview. He is quoted as saying, "Elon is acting like a spoiled child now, and he needs to grow up."

Jana and Elliot don't live with Errol, but they do have a family vibe. Jana still works and looks after her son, but the difference is, she has the total support of Errol both emotionally and financially. Given that their mother received absolutely no support when raising his children, it can come as no surprise that his older children aren't thrilled with their father's actions.

Maye Musk is quite happy to give interviews about herself, her career, and her successful kids, but she has maintained a dignified silence about her ex-husband. As a woman who has been described as an unconventional "it" girl, she has graced the covers of many magazines for over five decades. She has also received more highbrow accolades for her work in the field of nutrition. She glows with pride when she talks about her children and maintains that they are such strong, successful individuals because they suffered tough times when she was raising them as a single mom. "Poverty makes you work really hard," she said in an interview about her early life, a sentiment that is full of truth and pathos, unlike the glib description of childhood Errol Musk describes.

While it may seem that Elon Musk had a troubled childhood where he was bullied at school and home, it must be noted that his mother put her life on hold for her kids. Would he have had the same drive without her influence? Would he have been a different man if his family life had been happier? Nobody can know for sure.

Chapter 2: The Move to Canada

Following his troubled childhood, it is well documented that Maye Musk and her kids made a move to Canada when Elon was 17 years old. The family chose their new country due to the dual nationality of Maye, and Elon saw the move as a steppingstone to his final destination, the U.S.A. He was quoted in interviews that as a child, he noticed that the innovational tech ideas that would influence his thinking all came from the States. He wanted to make his way to California and saw Canada as the easier route to his dreams.

When he arrived in Canada, he was meant to live with his great uncle in Montreal before joining his mother and siblings in Toronto. He couldn't locate his relative and began his new life living in a cheap hostel and picking up part-time work. He then traveled to Saskatchewan to lodge with a second cousin. While there, he worked manual jobs at local farms and lumber mills.

In 1990, he gained entry to the Queen's University at Kingston, Ontario. Here he befriended a Canadian student who grew up in Geneva, and the pair of them shared an interest in strategy games. Musk wasn't accustomed to making friends, and Navaid Farooq shared memories of his time bonding with Elon playing the game Civilization while sharing the same dorm.

In the book "Elon Musk, the Quest for a Fantastic Future," he remembers his time in college and the long friendship he formed with Musk with fondness. He remembers a young man who was intense and quite serious about his college life. He recalls that Musk would often become lost in a project for hours and was able to filter out distracting information when immersed in work. He speaks of a kinship built on the ability to be alone and not feel socially awkward while in a busy environment.

In college, Elon was serious about his grades, and even though he found himself in a group of high achievers, he still stood head and shoulders above his classmates. Farooq talks candidly about the intense competition between the group following exams and tests. He recalls the moment following an economics exam that he realized just how advanced Musk was and the better understanding of the subject he displayed.

Of course, college is the place where Elon met his first wife, Justine. She also remembers their time dating as "very intense" and describes his insistence that things went his way. She calls her ex-husband the Terminator and describes his dating style as persistent. She said in an interview that Musk refused to give up. She always knew when it was him calling, as the phone ring persistently until she answered. She described his ability to lock his gaze on something and proclaim, "it will be mine."

Justine was one of the few students who were snapping on Musk's heels when it came to getting good grades, but even though the pair were in a relationship, he didn't give her any slack in the classroom. She remembers a psychology class they both took, and after the exam, they topped the class, with Justine receiving a score of 97 and Musk a score of 98. She recalls that while most students would have been more than happy with the score, Musk refused to accept the lost 2 points. He went to the professor and talked his way into a score of 100. He was always competing for that little bit extra.

Maybe the recollections of his former college friends will provide us with the most honest insight into the true character of Elon Musk and the intensity that drives him. In college, he had the characteristics that would soon transform a nerdy tech geek into one of the richest men in the world. He may only have spent three years in Canada, but he formed a bond that remains strong even today.

Chapter 3: Family Life: The Relationship History of Elon Musk

The beginning of the 21st century was an important turning point for Elon. He had obtained Canadian citizenship through his mother's nationality, and he moved to Kingston, Ontario to attend Queens University. While chilling in the dorm area, he spotted a beautiful young girl called Justine Wilson. He was a year ahead of her at school, but she was already writing for Marie Claire and making a name for herself in journalistic circles.

While Elon was keen to date Justine, she brushed him off to concentrate on her studies. He had asked her to join him for ice cream, and when she turned him down, he appeared at her dorm with two choc chip cones dripping down his arms. Eventually, the pair started dating, but it was never serious, and the pair separated after college. Wilson relocated to Japan for a year before returning to Canada, while Elon transferred to Wharton.

During their time apart, Musk would often send roses to his former girlfriend and the two kept in touch. They reconnected just as Elon was launching his first startup company and Justine was working on her first novel. Wilson is quoted as saying, "that once he called her, she realized just how much he meant to her, and the future of the relationship was sealed." He also recalls that his attempt to win her over was slightly more materialistic as he gave her his credit card to buy as many books for her research as she needed. Whatever the backstory, the pair married in 2000, and Musk began to attain serious wealth.

The couple then moved to Los Angeles and had their first son, Nevada, who they tragically lost to sudden infant death syndrome. The pair decided to use IVF to conceive, and they were blessed with twins Xavier and Griffin in 2004. Two years later, they used the treatment again to produce triplets, Kai, Saxon, and Damian. To the outside world, the family looked like the perfect unit, but behind closed doors, a deep void was growing between the couple.

Justine later said in an interview with Marie Claire that Elon was displaying "alpha male traits," and he was immersing himself in work. Although the pair were living a dream lifestyle filled with privilege and glamour, they began to drift apart as a couple. Justine and Elon attended marriage counseling, but even this couldn't save the troubled relationship, and the couple filed for divorce just a month later.

Just six weeks after filing divorce papers, Musk announced he was engaged to the actress Tallulah Riley. Surprisingly, Wilson has been quoted as saying that she got on well with Elon's new love interest, and the pair remain friends today. Musk has always proclaimed that the love he feels for his sons is the most important part of his life, and he would never treat them like his own father treated his children. The couple still shares custody, and they both spend the majority of their non-working hours with the boys.

Who is Tallulah Riley?

Elon Musk described his new love interest in an email to his ex-wife as a gorgeous British actress who is in her early 20s and has moved to LA to be with him. She also played one of the sisters in the 2005 version of Pride and Prejudice. Two years later, the pair were married amid a flurry of attention from the press.

The couple had met at a London nightclub in the West End named the Whisky Mist, where they were introduced to one another by the club promoter. Musk explained that he had reservations about the attractive actress, but his interest was piqued when she revealed her passion for electric cars and rockets. Soon after their first encounter, he proposed in true Elon Musk style! He gave her three engagement rings, an everyday one, a giant ring, and a diamond surrounded ring!

They married in September 2010 at a stunning castle in Scotland, yet the marriage lasted just two years. Even though they divorced quite quickly, the pair remained friendly, and

Musk tweeted his former wife, wishing her all the best and thanking her for an amazing four years.

After walking away with a reported $16 million divorce settlement, Riley continued with her career but didn't find the success she sought. The following summer, she remarried Elon, and the pair decided to give their love a second chance. In December 2014, Riley filed for divorce for a second time but later withdrew her application in the summer of 2015. The couple tried to make it work but finally made their divorce final in March 2016.

When asked to comment on their on-off relationship, Riley declared that Musk was her best friend and the love of her life. When asked if she would consider marriage for the third time, she refused to rule out the possibility. She stated that she still believed in marriage and its social construct and would never say never to another marriage with the billionaire. She was asked what the reason behind their marital woes, and she replied that putting her career on hold to loom after Musk's children was the biggest reason behind the marital tension.

Amber Heard and Elon Musk: What Really Happened?

Rumor has it that ever since 2013, Musk had developed a serious "thing" for the actress Amber Heard. He had made a cameo appearance in a movie she was starring in, but unfortunately for Musk, he failed to share a scene with her. The slightly obsessed Musk pestered the director and crew to set up a meeting with the actress, but she managed to dodge him on set. At the time, she was "seriously dating" Johnny Depp, who had left his long-term partner Vanessa Paradis to be with her.

Elon Musk is not a man who gives up easily. As Heard and Depp married in 2015, they were already stories of drunken fights and domestic violence from both partners. Also, Depp was away a lot, and it seemed that when Johnny was away, Amber would play! A security guard on duty at the penthouse that Heard and Depp lived in reported several occasions when he had seen the actress and the tech billionaire together when Depp was away filming.

Now fast forward to 2016 and the time following the split between Heard and Depp. Amber remained in the LA penthouse, and Johnny moved out. Pictures of Musk and Amber cuddling in the elevator were leaked to the press, and the pair finally revealed themselves as a couple.

Heard and Musk had a quite public affair, and he gave her a Tesla car as a gift. Unfortunately, Musk's gift came equipped with an extraordinarily successful tracking system that told Musk exactly where his girl was and who she was with. As the battle between Heard and Depp reached an intensity that was off the scale, Musk and Heard announced they were splitting up. They publicly blamed the split on their hectic schedules, but insiders believe that Elon wanted to distance himself from the whole Heard vs. Depp debacle.

The Current Mrs. Musk

Following the split with Heard, Musk revealed he hated being alone. When asked if he thought he tended to jump into relationships, he candidly replied that he found it hard to function when he was alone. He stated that going to sleep alone was his worst nightmare, and he craved the company of a long-term companion in his life.

In 2018 Elon met his current partner, the Canadian musician Grimes, and they now have a son called X AE A-12 or as his grandma calls him, X. They seem to be a match made in heaven as one source reports, "they are both as cuckoo as each other!" So, could this musical muse be the one? Only time will tell, but her varied background may give some clues to why the couple stands a better chance than most at being successful.

Grimes, real name Claire Boucher isn't just an experimental music artist; she also has a background in neuroscience and philosophy. She also harbored ambitions to join the space program, and she managed to take and pass all the requisite courses required before choosing to pursue a career in music.

Chapter 4: Zip2 - Elon's First Company

To Set the Scene

The year is 1995, and Elon Musk has just started his Ph.D. materials science course at Stanford. He has moved to San Francisco following his graduation from the University of Pennsylvania with a B.A. in Economics and a B.S. in Physics. He formerly attended the University of Pretoria for 5 months while waiting for his Canadian citizenship and has spent most of his adult life studying.

In Silicon Valley, the birth of the consumer internet was attracting interest from those in the know. A few weeks before Musk was due to start classes, the company Netscape went public with a valuation just short of $3 million. In the early days, this groundbreaking company dominated the internet browser field but was overtaken in the first browser war by Internet Explorer. The founder's Marc Andreessen and Jim Clark sparked the interest of Elon Musk, and he realized that he needed to get in on the action.

Musk attended just two days at Stanford before dropping out and deciding to build an internet company. Musk was reportedly inspired by an event during his internship in Silicon Valley in the summer of 1994. He had overheard an inept pitch from a Yellow

Pages rep, requesting an online listing that would reflect the printed book and help customers find a number. While the rep didn't get his point across, Musk was inspired by the thought of searchable web directories and the income they could generate. This idea stuck with Elon, and he decided to pursue it in 1995.

It is important to remember that in 1995 nobody could have imagined the impact that the internet would have on the world. Despite the success of Netscape and the growth of Silicon Valley, most people still thought the internet would turn out to be a passing fad. Elon invited his brother Kimbal to join him in California as his business partner, and the pair began to scheme. Another partner, Gregory Kouri, a friend of Kimbal's, joined the pair, and the idea of Zip2 began to form.

The company's mission was simple. Musk described it as a tool that made sure everyone would be able to find their nearest pizza shop and how to get there. It was described as an online version of Yellow Pages with maps. The idea may seem simple now, but back in 1995, the idea of computers being available in all households was a mere pipe dream. Luckily, the three young men could envision a time when this type of search would become an everyday part of life.

Elon had just $2000 in the bank, and his brother had a bit more after selling his share of a franchise he had been involved with, but finally, his father Errol came good, and he gave them

$28,000 to get the company going. Musk then purchased a local business directory for a couple of hundred dollars and approached a GPS company called Navteq to obtain free access to their software.

Following this, the concept was simple. He created the necessary coding and married the two databases. The product was created; the problem now was to convince businesses to subscribe. It may seem strange to us in the 21st century to imagine the difficulties the company had convincing small businesses to sign up. The trouble was they couldn't see the point, and the company failed to appeal to even the most daring venture capitalists.

With their ridiculously low start-up fund, the trio had to come up with a solution to get them through the developing stages. The two brothers decided that to invest their meager funds in the business, it meant sacrificing their home comforts. They slept on futons in the Zip2 office they had rented and showered at their local YMCA. Musk looks back on these lean times and jokes that it was the best physical shape he has ever been in!

The cutbacks weren't just applied to their personal life. The business was run on a small budget, with the two Musk brothers sharing just one computer. One of them would work during the day, and the other would work through the night. They started their business using the cheapest form of internet, an inexpensive dial-up modem, which was frustratingly slow but all they could afford. Fortunately, they convinced an Internet Service Provider in the office below them to let them piggyback their signal for a nominal fee. Elon drilled the hole himself and ran the cable down the stairs to hook up to the firm's internet.

Once the website was running smoothly and the brothers believed it was ready to market, they employed three salespeople to sell their product. The team worked on commission and began to trawl shopping malls and districts to find potential customers. The frugality of the company meant that as the business began to trickle in, the cash flow began rising and that appealed to investors. Finally, the venture capital community was starting to take notice of the emerging company, and Musk knew he had to grab the opportunity.

Elon knew that he needed to make an impression, and he set about using smoke and mirrors to do so! He built an impressive extension to case his humble computer and make it look like a supercomputer. The trick worked, and this futuristic look coupled with Musk's infectious enthusiasm secured him an investor. In 1996 the venture firm Mohr Davidow offered the young entrepreneur a $3-million investment.

Unfortunately, the money came with a list of conditions. Musk was demoted to the Head of Technology, and the reins of the company were handed over to a seasoned tech expert called Rich Sorkin. Musk and his partners were forced to hand over most of their shares in the company and take a back seat in the decisions foretelling which direction the company was headed.

With Sorkin at the helm, the company changed direction. They became the white knight to publishing and signed up the New York Times and other big media properties. They changed the focus of the business away from local outlets and instead chased the bigger companies. Craigslist was still a long way from robbing the major newspapers of their cash flow, but the writing was on the wall. The company grew quickly and began to attract attention from the best talents in Silicon Valley. While Musk was a talented coder, the initial work he had done was obviously the work of a self-taught programmer, and the company needed more professional help. The new engineers and coders formed an uneasy alliance with the original team, and while their efforts were successful, there was a great deal of friction within the ranks.

In 1998, things finally came to a head. Sorkin was convinced the company's future was with CitySearch, a national company that had a comparable business model but a wider reach. Musk initially agreed, but then decided that the strategies in place were compromising his initial vision for the company. He planned a coup to oust Sorkin and replace him with Musk as the CEO of Zip2, a place he had always believed was rightfully his. The plan worked at first until the board received an offer they just couldn't refuse. They were presented with an impressive offer of $307 million for the young company.

Musk had already tired of the company and took the offer he was given for his 7% share. At the age of 27, he walked away with a cool $22 million! Most people would consider Elon's time at Zip2 well spent, but when asked about the company, Musk looks back at the period with frustration and disappointment.

He recalls the time spent at Zip2 with self-reproach. He references mistakes made and claims to have made up for them in his future efforts. While he isn't specific about his regrets, most people have speculated that he was referring to his poor man-management and communication style.

Following his departure from Zip2, what did Musk do next? Well, he bought a new home and a flashy Maclaren car! He may have regretted his time at Zip2, but he now had some money to put towards his next venture.

Chapter 5: PayPal and the PayPal Mafia

In 1998, the emergence of digital payment and the platform we now know as PayPal occurred. The people who formed the company have since gone on to become some of the most influential people in the world of tech. This band of misfits may have been mismatched, but there is no argument about their brilliance in tech circles. The brand PayPal may have taken years to become the household name we know today, but it has become one of the most profitable in the world, and it deals with over 100 currencies across more than 200 world markets.

First, let's look at a timeline of the brand, and how it grew to become the leader in the e-commerce payment market. The history of PayPal may not be a long one, but it is filled with highs and lows as the company strived to convince its potential customers to trust them with their banking information. In the early years, they persuaded small businesses, emerging online sellers, and individual consumers to sign on and form a digital payment platform between sellers and consumers that hadn't been seen before.

At the start of the 21st century, the majority of online retail sites were still focusing on more traditional methods of payment and failed to see the potential of online payments. eBay and other retailers were still relying on checks and money orders to receive their payments, which meant that goods and services were delayed as they waited for clearance.

August 1998: Stanford University hosted a forum on the opportunities for global marketing, which saw key speeches from both Peter Thiel and Max Levchin, two of the most prominent founders of PayPal. Their meeting led to an idea for a "global wallet" that inspired them to reach out to other investors for support and ideas. Elon Musk had recently received $22 million from the sale of Zip2, and he used it to form a payment processing website called X.com.

December 1998: Thiel and Levchin merge their company, known as Confinity, with X.com and the PayPal mafia has its first three members. They decided to rename the company PayPal and set about using their entrepreneurial mindsets combined with their anti-establishment attitude to launch it on the digital market.

October 1999: The engineering department at PayPal develop an email-based payment option that increases its customer base significantly.

January 2000: As the 21st century begins, the founders and managers notice that their current subscribers are encouraging commercial outlets and other buyers to become PayPal users so they can get payments almost immediately. The founders recognized that the best way to boost their user base was to sign up eBay as a subscriber, and it proved to be successful as their user base reached and surpassed the million mark two months later.

June 2001: Although the brand PayPal has been used for the last 3 years, it is only in 2001 that the founders officially ditch the name Confinity and change it to PayPal.

February 2002: PayPal founders and managers decide to take the company public. The stock was offered at $13, and the IPO hit a high of $22.04 before closing for the day at $20.09. This was declared the best first day's trading gain for a new issue at the time.

October 2002: It is felt that a marriage between the extraordinarily successful auction site eBay and PayPal is needed, and the sale is agreed for $1.5 billion. Elon Musk opposed the sale but still walked away with $180 million to mark his time at PayPal. This enabled him to turn his attention to Tesla and SpaceX.

So, even though the connection with Elon Musk was severed, PayPal still went on to achieve amazing feats. In 2006 it achieved over 100 million end-user accounts and created PayPal mobile that encouraged users to make and receive payments using their smart devices. Their tenth anniversary in 2008 saw over 150 million users on the worldwide platform.

The next 6 years saw the PayPal brand grow and acquire more assets like Braintree Systems, which they purchased in 2013 for $800 million. This left PayPal as the number one competitor in the online payment market. There was trouble brewing, though, as one of their major shareholders, Carl Icahn, decided that the company needed to part ways with eBay.

This led to PayPal once again becoming a single trading company and floating its stock in July 2014. The market value soared as the trading day progressed and created an army of new millionaires referred to as "PayPal instant millionaires."

Between 2015 and 2017, PayPal went from strength to strength. Its subsidiary company Venmo passed a benchmark in online payments. In just one month, it processed over $1 billion, which was unheard of in previous trading history. In 2017, PayPal became a major voice in the peer-to-peer payment market. This type of payment meant that individuals could create transactions between themselves using individual accounts or cards through an online app. This meant that banks were taken out of the equation, and customers could expect a better rate of exchange without the traditional fees.

Following their first two decades of trading, PayPal is forging out into new markets. It has moved part of its focus to India, an important global market that has been neglected by other companies.

Other investments include a merging with Facebook to develop their Marketplace, and a huge investment in Uber to get a foothold in the rideshare market. PayPal will never be accused of sitting back and letting the market develop without them! They are still considered a major player in the global markets despite the emergence of serious competition.

What Happened to the PayPal Mafia?

While the story of PayPal is fascinating, what happened to the entrepreneurial founders once they left is even more incredible. Most people acknowledge that the so-called Mafia contained 23 members that at some time during its history played a major part in the success of PayPal.

The Don: The Founder Peter Thiel

Thiel started Confinity, which we of course know as the base company of PayPal. He served as CEO until the platform was acquired by eBay in 2002. It is reported that his 3.7% stake brought him a hefty $55-million payday.

In the years that followed, he became a huge player in the venture capital world. He was the first major outside investor in Facebook, and he also had ties to Yelp and LinkedIn. It may be argued that his greatest achievement was in 2005 when he helped to form the venture capital firm, Founders Fund. It invests in all stages and sectors of the market, including space innovations, AI, energy, and health.

The portfolio they hold is pretty impressive, with names like Airbnb, Spotify, and Lyft among their more well-known assets. They also pride themselves on their diversity and actively seek out underrepresented founders for every stage of their development.

The Godfather and Co-Founder: Max Levchin

Levchin was the man who made PayPal secure. When online payment platforms began to emerge, people were naturally wary of putting their details out there. As the company's chief technological officer, Levchin worked with David Gausebeck, the tech architect at the time, to develop the first version of CAPTCHA for PayPal users to prevent fraud.

Following his time at PayPal, Levchin served as chairman at Yelp from 2004 until 2015. Yelp is a public company that operates out of San Francisco. It helps to connect people with local businesses and offers a variety of career opportunities.

Currently, Levchin serves as CEO at Affirm, which is a layaway form of payment platform. It allows users to spread their payments over time when purchasing online products without paying huge interest rates. He also holds a position as chairman at Glow, an ovulation and period tracker that helps couples conceive more successfully.

Co-Founder: Ken Howery

Howery decided to stay on at PayPal after the 2002 sale to eBay, and he served as a director until 2003. He then formed ties with his old friend Peter Thiel and joined him on the board of Founders Fund, but the political world was calling, and Howery decided to answer that call! He is currently the US ambassador to Sweden and uses his business acumen to foster commercial and cultural relationships across the world.

Despite being one of the richest men in the world, Howery is active in several nonprofit operations, and is deeply involved with providing low-cost loans to low-income start-up firms.

Co-Founder: Luke Nosek

Nosek served as the VP of marketing and strategy at PayPal and followed his associates Peter Thiel and Ken Howery to Founders Fund. In 2017, he decided to launch his own investment fund named Giga fund that then helped raise capital to fund SpaceX. He is currently on the board at SpaceX and supports the company Research Gate which is an online resource for scientists and researchers to share their information and innovations.

The Firefighter: Reid Hoffman

During the early days of PayPal, many issues needed dealing with, and Hoffman served as an efficient part of that process. He left in 2002 following the sale and became a co-founder at LinkedIn. Hoffman also made early investments in prolific companies before joining the board of Microsoft in 2017. He is known as one of the most prolific angel investors operating in the tech world and is the author of many well-regarded start-up guides. He also hosts a podcast where he interviews successful company founders about how they achieved their success.

And so, the list goes on! Silicon Valley may seem like a vast arena for techies, but the truth is, wherever you look, you will likely find some kind of link to the early days of PayPal.

Chapter 6: Tesla: Saviors of the World or Toys for the Rich and Famous?

Whatever you think of Musk and his multiple companies, you would most certainly have heard of Tesla.

First, let's travel back to 1996 and have a look at the development team at General Motors. The concept for a fully electric car was under development, and the team was seeing a favorable reaction to their work. The program ran for three years and produced positive feedback from the test markets it used to produce their data. While the EV1 may have been considered an engineering success, the overall concept was deemed to be consigned to the history books, and the car was never released for sale to the public.

Four years later, these findings by General Motors inspired two engineers down in San Carlos, California to start their own electric car company. They may have been inspired by the GM engineers, but they named their company after the 19th century inventor, Nikola Tesla. Thomas Edison is famous for having discovered the power of direct current electricity, but Tesla developed "alternating current," which is the form transmission engineers still use today. And so, Tesla Motors was born.

Elon Musk was the face of the company from its conception, but he didn't officially join the company until 2004. The two original engineers, Martin Eberhard and Marc Tarpenning, were still serving as CEO and CFO, but Musk was providing the financial support the company needed. He invested $30 million of his own money and encouraged other substantial investments from Google and other sources.

In 2006, the prototype for the Tesla Roadster was unveiled, and the world was introduced to the first fully electric sports car. The concept was unveiled at a 350-person invitational event at Santa Monica in July and later appeared at auto shows in LA, Detroit, and SF. The company also unveiled its idea as far away as Frankfurt, Germany.

The Roadster was a revelation in the field of electric motors. Tesla had achieved the first entirely electric car that had a practical battery that could be recharged from standard electrical outlets. The car could travel for over 250 miles on a single charge and had an acceleration rate and top speed that was comparable to other popular sports cars on the market.

So, why don't we all have a Roadster sat on our drive today? Although it was a huge success, there were problems with the car. The charging time was between 24 and 48 hours on a basic home outlet, and the original models were priced at over $100,000.

This made them unavailable for most consumers, and only the rich and famous were buying them to begin with.

The problems with the prototype weren't the only ones the company had to deal with. There were internal wrangles between the heads of the company, and this was reflected by important changes that were made at the senior level. 2007 saw Eberhard resign as CEO and take a seat on the advisory board. He was succeeded by an investor in the company who served as a temporary CEO while the company searched for a more permanent person for the job. In November 2007, that man materialized in the form of Ze'ev Drori.

Who is Ze'ev Drori?

This Israeli-born entrepreneur founded Monolithic Memories in 1970 and was responsible for inspiring and game-changing developments in memory and logic technology. He oversaw the merge of Monolithic Memories with Advanced Micro Devices ten years later for an eye-watering value of over $400 million. During his time at MM, he also acquired the fledgling company Clifford Electrics which was responsible for innovative work in car security systems.

He developed the company to incorporate the latest tech straight out of Silicon Valley to become the key player in remote car alarms. The growth of the company was phenomenal, and they soon dominated both the foreign and domestic markets.

He is known as an avid car driver and has taken part in Formula Cars since 1997, so coupled with his 30 years' experience in the tech and auto world, he seemed like the perfect candidate to become CEO of Tesla.

In 2007 the Roadster project had lagged, and many people credit Drori with refocusing attention and manufacturing its subsequent launch in 2008. Just before this successful launch, the two founding members of the company left and cut all ties with Tesla. Musk then became the CEO in 2009, with Drori becoming Vice-Chairman. The changes weren't met with universal approval within the company, and Musk stamped his authority on the team by sacking 25% of the staff.

Eberhard and Tarpenning were also refusing to lie down quietly. They claimed they had been unfairly ousted from the company and subjected to libel and slander from the new CEO. Unfortunately, they failed to make their allegations stick, and the lawsuits were dropped later that year.

Despite the seemingly successful launch of the Roadster, the company was experiencing cash flow issues, leading to potentially less available cash than needed to deliver the cars they had already sold. The company needed help, and this came in the form of a direct loan from the D of E to make sure the company could survive and carry-on trading. Tesla also sold 10% of the company to Daimler for $50 million.

In 2008, the company pledged to make its future products more accessible to the average person. It promised a 25% reduction in price for the Roadster and the production of a more traditional style of car. Arguably this took place in 2011, when the newest offering of Tesla was revealed in the form of the Model S sedan. The car of the people was still a luxurious sedan, but it signaled the first step toward the mainstream consumer market.

The Model S was well received, and it won awards from automotive and environmental sources alike. It had significant advances to the Roadster with a shortened charging time and a longer running time thanks to the improved batteries it used. The company also traded on the popularity of the brand with their customers. In 2012, it developed charging stations referred to as "Superchargers" and placed six of these charging stations throughout California, offering free charging to all Tesla owners. The company then began to distribute the stations worldwide, reducing charging times to all owners of electric and hybrid vehicles.

2013 saw an uptick in the company's fortunes as it announced its first profits ever. The tide had turned for Tesla Motors, and the future looked bright. They announced the construction of its Gigafactory in Nevada, which heralded the era of development of batteries. Musk realized that these crucial components would revolutionize the whole business model and open ambitious avenues in alternative energy.

2015 saw Musk launching a new line of products that were a world away from his beloved motor cars. These solar energy products were designed to introduce renewable energy into homes and businesses across the globe using rechargeable batteries. By 2017, he decided to change the name of the company to reflect his broader ambitions in the renewable energy space, and Tesla Motors became Tesla Inc.

Of course, the company hadn't turned its back on the motor industry altogether. In 2016, Musk announced the production of the Model 3 sedan. It would be the first all-electric car available below the $70,000 price mark and was designed to appeal to the mainstream car market. This was also the beginning of a pattern between the overexcited Musk and his sweeping public statements that would occasionally land the company in hot water. He announced to the world that the company would deliver around 200,000 vehicles in 2017 when, in reality, the company could only produce around 50,000.

The truth was even direr in 2018. Production of the Model 3 was minimal. In 3 months, the company produced just 2,400 cars despite promising 5,000 per week. When questioned by consumers and investors, Musk referred to the problems created by the supply chain, which meant they had to rely on other sources for parts rather than building and assembling the cars in the same location.

The problems with production would seem insignificant compared to the legal troubles Musk would stir up later that year. 2018 was the year that Musk used his Twitter platform to announce that Tesla was about to go private, and he quoted the stocks at $420 per share. Unsurprisingly this led to a flurry of trading that drove the price of Tesla stock up, leading to unwanted attention from the U.S. Securities and Exchange Commission. It was reported that Musk had used false and misleading statements on a public forum to boost the stock of his company. They accused the CEO of Tesla of securities fraud and fined the company and Musk $20 million.

Musk stepped down from his position as Chairman of the Board following the settlement, and he was replaced by Robyn Denholm. Tesla also pledged to keep a close eye on the Twitter account of Musk and make sure he behaved in a more befitting manner regarding the company.

Despite settling with the SEC back in 2018, the agency sought a contempt order claiming that Tesla didn't monitor the statements issued by Musk regarding production rates. The settlement was revised after a judge ruled that the company had been remiss about Musk's outbursts on social media.

2019 wasn't all bad news for Tesla and its enigmatic leader! In November, they announced their latest product, the Cybertruck. Designed to look like a cross between a DeLorean and the Lotus model from a James Bond film, it is the latest entry into the electric truck market. Musk unveiled the truck in his own inimitable style with a Tesla employee attempting to smash the exterior with a sledgehammer. He claimed the windows of the Cybertruck were made of transparent metal and are impervious to bullets.

What happened next was unbelievable. The world press was treated to a scene that would prove priceless. Elon Musk invited one of its key designers to try to crack one of the windows with a steel ball. He then threw the ball at the side window of the truck, and a network of spiderweb cracks appeared. Unfazed, Musk instructed the engineer to try the same thing at the rear window. The same thing happened, and the window cracked. This led to an iconic image of Elon Musk conducting the rest of the presentation stood in front of a truck with two broken windows!

When asked about the incident, Musk explained that he had compromised the windows of the truck by hitting the bodywork with a sledgehammer. He then said that in the future, he would throw the steel ball first and then sledgehammer the doors! Luckily, it didn't seem to harm the image of the company or the truck as Tesla continues to grow in popularity.

Despite facing some issues early on, Tesla has grown to become one of the major players in the automotive industry. In fact, Tesla is one of the few companies that have thrived during the coronavirus pandemic, but will it still be a major player in the future? Obviously, that will depend heavily on the decisions of Elon Musk, but it appears that Tesla is only going to grow in popularity, products, and profits!

Chapter 7: SpaceX: Is it the Future of Space?

There aren't many people who haven't heard of this revolutionary corporation founded by Elon Musk. Commonly referred to as SpaceX, its full name is Space Exploration Technologies Corporation, and was founded in 2002. Musk has proclaimed the company is ushering in the new era of commercial spaceflight by producing renewable methods of traveling to space. Space travel is notoriously expensive, and the rockets and capsules involved are only usable for one journey. Musk and SpaceX are working on reusable rockets accompanied by cheaper satellites and engines.

Space Travel

Elon was born in 1971, and he grew up amid promises of space-age communities with huge space scrapers designed to accommodate the growing human population. The media images of the time were households with robot servants and streets filled with flying cars. The film industry was fueling the public's imagination with images of the 21st century with 2001 A Space

Odyssey filling living rooms with promises of advanced technology and space travel.

The Moon was now seen as an extension of Earth. The government and NASA were setting goals to send manned missions to Mars with the idea that it could be colonized in the future. Images of Space shuttles filled the news, and even the tragic shuttle Challenger in 1986 failed to dampen the enthusiasm for space.

Musk's generation grew up with Star Trek and Star Wars, providing them with a narrative for the future. As time went on and the USA began to work with Russia to explore the options that space offered, and the 21st century saw the first permanent crew on the International Space Station, Musk was becoming successful in other fields. In 2001 The US millionaire Dennis Tito became the first space tourist and spent a week in orbit visiting the Space Station and taking a ride on a Russian spacecraft.

Elon Musk is a visionary and a 21st Century renaissance man. He has the ambition to "fix" the planet, but he also realizes the importance of a plan B. He believes that humanity is at risk from natural forces, and he understands that the solar system we live in could be the resource that saves us. He believes that traveling to other planets will help our civilization spread out and avoid obliteration caused by a single disaster.

With his other projects, he is doing his best to create a more stable climate and provide sustainable energy, therefore, promising a brighter future for the younger generation. Musk has the skills and imagination to turn the current climate around and make the planet a cleaner place, but he also recognizes that other options should be in place.

In 2002 Musk formed SpaceX to help space travel become more accessible. He had conceptualized a project in the previous year to land a greenhouse on the planet Mars and attempt to grow produce. He planned to pledge money to help NASA reignite the public's interest in all things relating to space and what lies beyond Earth. He traveled to Russia to purchase cheap rockets and spare rocket parts but returned without success. He found that all the rockets available were just too expensive for the projects he had in mind.

Upon his return from Russia, he decided the best course of action would be to start his own rocket-building company, as thus, SpaceX was born!

SpaceX Timeline

2002: The Merlin and the Kestrel engines were designed by SpaceX for propulsion. The Merlin is designed to be used on their launch vehicle and for sea rescues. It is fueled by liquid oxygen and incorporates an injector style turbo pump that is based on the original type of engine used in the Apollo program. The Kestrel is designed to be the second stage engine and lacks a turbopump. The names of the engines are derived from American birds of prey.

Several launch vehicles were also developed in this first year of research, including the Draco control vehicle and the Dragon craft designed to transport cargo into space. SpaceX became the first commercial company to fly humans to the International Space Station on the craft Dragon2.

2004: Work began on designing the Falcon 1 rocket. Musk appeared before a government subcommittee and he submitted his ideas for the first reusable orbital rocket. On June 21st, Virgin and Scaled Composites sent Spaceship One into orbit to become the first privately funded manned space flight.

2005: An announcement was made that SpaceX would commit to a program based on human-related space travel that would be in place for at least the next five years. It released plans for a spacecraft called the Dragon, which showed a conventional capsule designed to carry up to seven humans per journey.

2006: In March, the company made its first launch of the Falcon 1 spacecraft. All appeared well until a leak ended the launch with a huge fire. Despite this failure, the company garnered massive interest and received millions of dollars' worth of business. 2006 was also the year that NASA invited bids for the maintenance of the ISS and possible crew transport following the decision to decommission the government-funded space shuttle. SpaceX was granted the contract ahead of all its rivals and was paid $396 million to fund the development of the Dragon craft, while the company itself pledged over $500 million to develop the Falcon project.

2008: Following two previously unsuccessful attempts to achieve orbit, Falcon 1 became the first privately funded rocket to attain orbit status. It is also the first rocket to be fueled by the much cheaper liquid oxygen. In August, the company accepted a huge investment from the Founders Fund, an organization run by some of Elon Musk's former co-founders at PayPal.

2009: Another first for the company occurred in this year as they launched a satellite in Earth's orbit.

2010: This was the year SpaceX unveiled a new spacecraft, the Falcon 9. It was launched in June and was successful on its first attempt. SpaceX also became the first commercial company to retrieve a spacecraft successfully. They launched, deployed, and then controlled a re-entry with the Dragon spacecraft, signaling the emergence of the first reusable spacecraft ever. The company broke ground on the development that would become the launch site for the much-heralded Falcon 9. The company issued a statement that this development would be the first to smash the $1,000 per pound cost of orbiting and make it more cost-effective to transport humans through the solar system.

2011: NASA released figures to confirm that SpaceX had developed their spacecraft and technology at a fraction of the cost it would have cost the agency. SpaceX also began the development of the Falcon Heavy, a reusable lift and launch vehicle that would be a part of the development of the Falcon 9 program.

2012: To mark the 10th anniversary of its founding, figures were released that showed the level of funding from private equity, Musk himself, and other investors. The Dragon became the first commercial craft to successfully dock with the ISS. NASA revealed that they have awarded SpaceX a $440 million grant for further research.

2013: The Dragon spacecraft developed problems with its engine while in orbit and partially lost control of its movements. Engineers were able to repair the engines and resolve issues from Earth, and the spacecraft resumed its mission and successfully reached the ISS.

2014: SpaceX revealed the Crew Dragon. This variant of the original Dragon craft is solely designed to carry humans to the ISS. The technology enabled the craft to use precision water landings to return to Earth and made it the first craft to offer multiple usages with a higher degree of certainty. The cost for each astronaut's seat was around $23 million compared to $76 million per seat on the Russian Soyuz. NASA immediately booked four separate flights per year.

2015: A Falcon 9 first stage launch returned successfully to Earth. SpaceX raised $1 billion of funding from Google and Fidelity, which saw its company's valuation soar to around $12 billion. SpaceX also announced the first-ever competition and built a test track to hold the Hyperloop event.

2016: SpaceX began using drone ships for rocket landings. The company also won the first national security launch ever awarded to a commercial company. A private customer placed an order to fly around the Moon in 2023 in the newly commissioned craft named the Starship. The company announced that the Starship would be the first usable passenger craft by the early 2020s.

2017: SpaceX formed a subsidiary company called the Boring Company. Initially, the company concentrated on the construction of short adjoining tunnels to facilitate testing. Research on the development of Super Draco engines was also announced. A plan was announced to fund a low-cost Mars based research mission to bring back samples from the planet for studies.

2018: The Falcon Heavy was successfully launched. Musk placed his personal Tesla Roadster onboard the spacecraft and declared it to be the most powerful rocket on Earth, which he demonstrated by sending his car into space. The first astronauts to board the Crew Dragon were also announced in this year.

2019: SpaceX stated that they were required to lay off a percentage of their workforce to fund research into new projects. The Crew Dragon completed its first successful trip to the ISS.

2020: The first crewed mission involving the Crew Dragon took place on the 20th of May and transported two astronauts to the ISS. The cargo Dragon completed its 100th successful mission to the space station.

Of course, much more has happened during the last 18 years, but the timeline provided above shows the main body of achievements the corporation has completed. The main thing to take away from the SpaceX phenomenon is the affordability it has provided compared to government agencies. While they've made great progress in a short period of time, Musk is no way near satisfied, and has his eyes set on the goal of colonizing Mars.

Chapter 8: Neuralink and AI

Elon Musk is always one step ahead of his competitors when it comes to tech innovations, but is Neuralink a step too far? The Corporation was founded in 2016 and has its headquarters in San Francisco. The idea behind Neuralink is to implant micron-scale threads into the human brain that are attached to a device called the Link that is placed behind the ear. The electrodes within the threads are designed to detect neural signals and create a brain-computer interface.

This would allow the wearer to control technology simply by thinking about it. The implantable wireless device would be inserted into the brain using a robotic system controlled by neurosurgeons as the threads cannot be inserted by human hands. The system is powered by an external charger that wirelessly connects to the implant to provide a charge from outside the body.

The user would then install the Neuralink app that will guide them through the exercises they need to master before they can control their devices. Once these procedures are in place, the user can control any mouse or keyboard they choose and experience the realistic connection without intervention and in high definition.

This innovative product is referred to as a BMI or brain-machine interface. They can help people who are paralyzed to control tech, and they can also send information back to the brain and restore any damaged functional areas. For instance, if someone has lost their sense of touch, the BMI can rewrite the information needed to make the brain restore function.

This idea may sound like something straight from a sci-fi plot, but the idea has already been developed to help people with disabilities and to treat Alzheimer's patients. So, what is different about Elon Musk's development of the BMI? He believes that it is needed to secure humanity's future. He believes that the advancing technology behind artificial intelligence can leave mankind behind and make humans benign. He maintains that even the lowest level of AI will soon make normal human interactions obsolete.

What Types of BMI Are Out There?

It may come as a surprise to know that this kind of research has been around for decades. Cochlear ear implants have been used for years to treat patients with severe hearing loss.

How Does a Cochlear Implant Work?

This type of implant is vastly different from a hearing aid. Standard aids amplify the external sounds to make the ears work more efficiently. Implants bypass the damaged areas of the ear and connect directly to the auditory nerve within the brain. The sounds generated by cochlear implants vary from "normal" sounds, and the patient must relearn how to distinguish what they are hearing. These types of implants received FDA approval in the mid-1980s and have been used to help children over the age of 12 months who are deaf or severely hard of hearing.

Adults who lose their hearing later in life can also benefit from the implants, but children find it easier to adapt to the sounds they are hearing as they have no historical references to confuse them. Studies have shown that young children following an intense therapy course coupled with a cochlear implant can develop language skills at the same rate as children with regular hearing.

There is a BMI equivalent that is used to treat patients with Parkinson's disease called Deep Brain Stimulation or DBS. While the optimal treatment for Parkinson's is still medication, this type of therapy can help patients to improve motor symptoms.

How Does the DBS System Work?

The treatment involves a pulse generator that is similar to a pacemaker under the epidermis around the chest or stomach. This generator is then connected to the brain using fine wires. Once the device is activated, it delivers a high-frequency signal to the brain, which alters the messages in the brain that cause the symptoms of the disease.

Unlike the cochlear implants, this type of treatment does involve surgery, and there are risks attached to the procedure. It must be noted that DBS is not a cure and is only used to lessen symptoms when conventional medication isn't proving effective.

There are also some less invasive BMI's available already that don't involve surgery. These types of brain-computer interfaces are known in the industry as wearables.

How Do Wearables Work?

These are usually non-invasive and come in the form of a headband, hat, or wristband with the device interwoven. When activated, they then receive signals from the brain that are like the responses a doctor gets when performing an EEG scan. The signal can also be sent via the wearable to the brain, but the interfaces have a significantly weaker response than the postsurgery options. The signal is good enough to cause a yes/no response from the brain but can't control tech.

Companies like Kernel and Ctrl Labs are already developing these types of wearables to help patients with relevant medical conditions. Products like the Flow 50 and the Kernel Flow are described as the most effective forms of non-invasive brain interface technology that connect via USB-C and have over 1,000 pairs of source directors. The Emotiv wireless EEG brain wear is designed to be simple to use, with software that measures brain data and adjusts when required.

Some companies like Neurosky have recognized that non-invasive BMIs can be used to interact with games and everyday tech but are limited to simple responses from avatars within a game. For instance, your movements would be restricted to a simple jump or push command, unlike the Neuralink technology that offers a much more interactive experience.

Drawbacks of Neuralink Technology

As with all groundbreaking innovations, there is bound to be some hand wringing and dismissive comments from experts and scientific bodies, but it cannot be dismissed off-hand just as it cannot be embraced unequivocally. Neuralink could potentially be the next step in human development. It would allow users to become connected at a biological level to the internet.

As humans, we would be able to share all our thoughts, hopes, and fears with the world in a millisecond. There would be no need to use speech or text to transmit our thoughts; they would simply appear. Is this a natural evolution for the human race, or is it simply one step too far? The legal and moral implications are endless, but is that a solid enough reason to dismiss the concept?

Consider the Evolution of Humanity

- Man discovers fire and makes the first tools

- They then develop the first forms of oral language

- This is then developed into writing, and early alphabets are formed

- Man finds a way of printing language and sharing it with others

- Man discovers electricity

- This develops into telephones, radios, and other media devices

- Personal computers and smartphones are available

- Virtual reality is developed and used to augment our interactions

When you consider the facts, a whole-brain interface seems like the next step in the evolution of man. Having access to the outside world through your thoughts would logically be the next step, so why are people worried?

1) The question is, do we need to have intrusive surgery for a nonmedical reason to keep up with AI? Brain surgery is a serious procedure that involves risks that are both long and short term. Should we really be considering it just to connect to the internet?

2) Who will have access to the data we receive? Who will govern what we can and can't see? Will we be bombarded with advertising and manufactured "news" that is designed to change our thought patterns?

3) What will it cost? Is there a danger that this type of technology will only be available to the members of society who are super-wealthy? Will this mean they have yet another advantage over the rest of us?

4) How will the software affect our personalities? Will the constant flow of information cause us to overload and create mental health issues?

5) Who oversees security? Will we be leaving ourselves open to hacking?

6) Smart tech also means exploitable. If you have ever been subject to online hacking or a breach of data, then you know the pain of this type of crime.

7) Will the technology require a whole new field of laws? Is this the dawn of the Cognitive police?

No matter what your personal thoughts are on the technology and the questions that surround it; you can't ignore it and hope it will go away! Musk has already proved his brilliance and his ability to ruffle the feathers of formidable players on the global stage, but is that what's happening here? The truth is there are no major players in this field, at least for now. His former operations have always been creating innovations in a more established industry. He has been involved with the oil and gas industries, the car industry, and the complex world of the military, but Neuralink is a whole new ball game.

One thing is for sure; having Neuralink in this emerging field will encourage the industry to grow. Companies who may have been unaware of this type of research may now be interested in getting involved in the industry, and that can only be good for the field. Any innovation that has the name Elon Musk attached to it will always attract public attention and media coverage. Judging from his previous developments, Musk is also known for his long-term commitment to projects, both physically and financially.

The field of BMI and wearables may seem like a lifetime away, but Musk himself has declared that he sees the technology being available to the masses by 2028. He also predicts that the procedure of having the implant will be as simple and automated as laser eye surgery.

Chapter 9: What Does the Future Hold?

As a new father and one half of a successful couple, Musk is probably more settled at home than he has ever been in the past. Does this mean we can expect to see less of him in the future as he takes a back seat in his business dealings and concentrates on family life? Chances are, we can see the exact opposite. Musk has often said that he works better when his relationship status is loved up!

Before the pandemic, Musk was filled with ideas and innovations for the future. He was focused on producing a compact SUV called the Model Y, and despite the troubles that 2020 produced, deliveries of the compact crossover began in March 2020.

The Tesla Roadster is also thought to be making a reappearance with improvements made to the current model 3 that is reported to be over 4 times as efficient as the original model. Tesla has also unveiled plans to create a Gigafactory in China in 2021 with plans to produce electric vehicles there shortly after. China has already pledged to have more electric vehicles on the road by 2030, and Tesla will play a major part in making this happen. Alongside the Gigafactory, there are plans for over 1,000 superchargers in China.

SpaceX also has big plans for the future. 2022 is the planned date for a cargo mission to Mars. Musk has plans to use his revamped Starship spaceship that is codenamed the Big Falcon Rocket to travel to the Red Planet and open avenues of space travel that have formerly been unimaginable. The BFR will attempt to confirm that there are sufficient water resources on the planet and identify any hazards. It will carry and deploy power mining equipment and life support infrastructure ready for manned space flights that will follow.

2023 will see the lunar circumnavigation mission called the #dearMoon project. This will be a private flight designed to promote lunar tourism and is classed as an art project. The collaboration between Musk's SpaceX and Japanese billionaire Yusaku Maezawa will take a painter, musician, film director, and fashion designer onboard the spaceship. The thought behind the mission is that if Picasso, Lennon, and other creative giants had been able to see the moon up close and personal, it would have inspired their work to even greater heights.

2024 is the year SpaceX is planning to follow up the cargo flights with manned missions and begin the process of colonizing Mars. The plan is to send two separate manned flights to begin work on the Martian colony. The first set of astronauts will be tasked with constructing a fuel plant that will form the beginning of the new colony. The second set of settlers will begin to build multiple landing pads and then begin to create an urban environment.

The goal of the project is to create a city that has an environment that is suitable for human settlers to live comfortably. When asked what the city will look like, Musk replied, "Life in glass domes at first" and then expressed his belief that terraforming will be a process that is too slow to be relevant in his lifetime. His plans to establish a base could be the first step to the formation of a future spacefaring civilization.

Musk believes that getting to Mars isn't an issue anymore, but he does acknowledge that building a self-sustaining city on Mars comes with its own set of problems.

The other contenders in the race to populate Mars and promote space tourism may feel that Musk has attracted attention for the wrong reasons. The truth is that any projects associated with this larger-than-life character will always make headlines. Surely this is a good thing when a project or idea is so controversial. The more we understand the difficulties and expectations such projects are subject to then the more we understand the possible timelines for their completion.

So, what about his personal life? Any changes there? Well, in true Musk style, in April 2020, Elon Musk announced to the world that he thought that Tesla's stock price was too high, and he was selling off all his worldly possessions! He tweeted over a dozen tweets in just over an hour with his "news" about his take on the property market and his plans to sell almost all his personal possessions.

The one thing we can be sure of is Elon Musk is not going to disappear from the public eye any time soon. His personality and business acumen means that there is still a lot to expect from this enigmatic man. Love him or loathe him, you can't ignore that Musk is one of the luminaries of the 21st century, and he isn't going anywhere. The world would be a duller place if Elon decided to retire or fade into the background, so we should embrace him and give thanks that there are characters like him with vision and the courage to follow through on ideas that others would dismiss.

Conclusion

No matter what you feel about Musk, it is a safe bet that at least one company he is or was associated with has some impact on your life. He has been called many things, a visionary, an egoist, and the real-life Tony Stark, but he survives his harshest critics. Now that you know his history and the influences that have formed his personality, you can now make an informed decision about Elon Musk and the role he is playing in the history of the 21st Century.

Thank you for taking the time to read this book. I hope you have enjoyed learning about the entrepreneurial icon, Elon Musk.

References

Business Insider. (2019). Business Insider. http://www.businessinsider.com

Cleantech News — #1 In EV, Solar, Wind, Tesla News. (n.d.). CleanTechnica. from http://www.cleantechnica.com

Futurism | Science and Technology News and Videos. (n.d.). Futurism. from http://www.futurism.com

International: Top News And Analysis. (2016, September 27). CNBC. http://www.cnbc.com

Maggie Johnson - All About Clint Eastwood's Ex-Wife. (n.d.). Facts Ninja. from http://www.factsninja.com

MEAWW - Media, Entertainment, Arts, WorldWide. (n.d.). Meaww.com. from http://www.meaww.com

Newsweek. (2019). Newsweek. http://www.newsweek.com

Psychology Today Canada: Health, Help, Happiness + Find a Therapist CA. (2019). Psychology Today. http://www.psychologytoday.com

Stock Market - Business News, Market Data, Stock Analysis. (n.d.). TheStreet. http://www.thestreet.com

The News Wheel. (n.d.). The News Wheel. from http://www.thenewswheel.com